# Confluences:
Indian Women, Indian Goddesses

# Confluences:
## Indian Women, Indian Goddesses

by

nishi chawla

INDIALOG PUBLICATIONS PVT. LTD.

Published in October 2007

Indialog Publications Pvt. Ltd.
O - 22, Lajpat Nagar II
New Delhi - 110024
Telefax: 91-11-29835221/29830504
www.indialog.co.in



10 9 8 7 6 5 4 3 2 1

Printed at Brijbasi Art Press Limited.



ISBN 81-8443-018-3

*To my mother*
*who passed away on April 3, 2007,*
*leaving me with a void, while she gave me the space,*
*filled with so much mothering.*

## CONTENTS


| | |
|---|---|
| Ila's Message | 11 |
| Sita's Divinity | 13 |
| Almost two sisters, almost Sita and Mary | 15 |
| Sita In Her Exile | 17 |
| Sita's Red Riding Hood | 19 |
| Durga Power | 21 |
| The Blackness of Kaali | 24 |
| To Lakshmi | 26 |
| Draupadi's Angst | 28 |
| Mira Bai's Aubade | 30 |
| Parvati's Penance | 32 |
| Amba's *Swayamwara* | 34 |
| *Ganga Maiyya* or Mother Goddess | 36 |
| Gandhari's Blindfolded Life | 38 |
| Urmila's Protest | 40 |
| The Texture of Devaki's life | 41 |
| Kunti's Secret Mantra | 43 |
| Duty-Bound Uma | 44 |
| Bhairavi the Terrible | 46 |
| Almost Two Sinners, Shabari and Mary Magdalene | 48 |
| Mandodhari's Grief | 50 |
| Is Shurpanakha a Dalit Woman? | 52 |

Rohini the Favorite 54
Kausalya, The Co-Wife 56
Annapurna's Food Fixation 58
Because my Great-Grandmother Refused to Become *Sati* 60
Noor Jehan's song to a *Purdah* Woman 62
Her Survival Kit 64
Upon Sighting the Moon 66
Her Desires, The Desiring Woman 68
Did She Eat A Bite Of Eve's Apple? 70
Tell me, how was it sleeping with him, your real man? 72
She Does Not Play With A Barbie Doll 74
When Savitri's Daughter must file for Divorce 76
My Indian Sappho/The Sappho in Me 79
Repressions and Confessions 81
When Sita is Beaten up Everyday 83
A Modern Woman's Work Strip-Tease 85
A Small Kitchen Fire 87
As an Indian Spinster Would 89
Anaarkali's Dance 91
The Fire Queen of Jhansi 93
An Old Bag Is Not An Old Hag 95
Her Inheritance 97
My Papa's Conundrum:
From a Daughter to her Dead Father 99
A Daughter-in-law's Guilt 101
This Mother-To-Be Visits an Abortion Clinic 102
Bollywood Goddesses 104
The Inside Passage of Sisterhood 106
To My Mother 108
The Story of Indian Women, Indian Goddesses 110

*How important it is for us to recognize and celebrate*
*our heroes and she-roes!*
— Maya Angelou

## Ila's Message

Married to one who performed the sacrifice, the son of God who
breaking the earth upon the palm of his hand, throwing the grain
into the gut of the sputtering flames, their ripening gold disturbed
by their own devouring, licking the listless ashes,
trembling the root life awake, the angels and the gods,
the sun, the earth, man and woman, child and messenger.
Then celebrate the same blood drops.

Tickling the ribs of the tongue with eager passion,
skinning the thick hide of the earth with its coral truths,
waiting for the soul to carve itself out a space that lingers,
then gathering the pieces in its chaste chest, bundled together,
piercing the shaking silence with its own silences,
swallowed whole thoughts, teeth gnashing,
gushing, its teeth and its tongue. Breaking.

Those live moments, when she turns into the pearly nourishment
of a shade resembling a woman. She must then swallow the venom
of worthless weeds pulling her down. Slipping under their wet feet,
until they fall, and fall, unfold like the rawness of her edible vulva,
and turning into a man, like fruit that moistens in slow steps,
the sound of its translucent gurgling drowns it out.
Streaming along the perforations of its own saddened earth,
gently tapping the lost towers on the hillside,

scattering its seeds along the fertile shanks of lost memory,
pouring it down communion's channels, tasting
the temerity of time, its invidious juices bundled together,
then release, like something swiftly passed, ejaculated,
then diving, conniving, disrupting its own disappearance.

This is the way to that God who leaves no witness
of its own gendered remains, says Ila.

---

* Ila in Sanskrit refers to the wife and daughter of Vaivasmata Manu. By the decree of Saraswati, she is one month a woman and the other, a man. This may be an allusion to the androgynous second race. Ila also means the flow of speech.

## Sita's Divinity

That little one that I am, I look quizzical
and wonder upon my divine essence.
The white potter takes a lump of brown clay,
discretely molds and shapes the pliable lump
to a human shade that he alone desires.

While firing the brown clay in the gray kiln,
he shapes it black and then reshapes it blacker
until he meets his own black desires.
That image that he creates of me,
is firm now, centuries have eroded,
I remain fixed, undressing me is only a ritual.

I grow into a colorful universe. It is no treachery,
to show my flesh in any color. I am incarnate
in the woman who bears a child year after year,
and one who never will. I wear a red sari, my redness
bloody as sunken stars. The white veil disappears
in the black *burka* that I must wear all the time.

Since I cherished an ideal, I must be the ideal one.
I am the mother and I am the daughter. I must be the wife
and I must be the one who cannot. The potter stuck two mounds
across me, and then slit me up and down, so I must

embellish the truth about me. The blood drops that I shed,
month after month, dry my tears-driven ceremonies.

That voice that I may have, he has slaughtered into a thousand;
so I speak many languages, and am known in many more.
Someone sings for me too, and those songs have a kindred tongue.
I, too sing, for I am Sita.

I am the victim and I am the victimizer.
I am the earth goddess, my healing reaches back to my self.
I am the earth woman, my humanness reaches back to my being.
I am your ancestor, my divine being reaches back to you.

* Sita, the wife of Rama, has been worshipped in various guises.

## Almost two sisters, almost Sita and Mary

I've not known seas.
I've not known seas older than this earth and older than
the heart that throbs within me.

I sing "Ave Maria" and wonder what it means
to crush my child to my golden bosom
until it spills all its gold. I then light
a candle and turn my soul to the East.

I sit on a red lotus and look around me.
My ten eyes and five heads can turn all around.
I hear the sea churn. I hear it mix some nectar
with a dash of cosmic poison, a little moonlight,
and the branch of a tree. I meditate. *Dheemahi.*
Upon two foundling sisters, two earth goddesses,
one sprung from a furrow in a field freshly ploughed,
and the other from soil past bearing any fruit.

I bathe in ancient seas that sprung an immaculate
conception on one. The other looked upon two,
not one son, as her own. But I still hear them
singing. Together in their sisterly moments,
they sit on that hammock, while the wind whistles,
strums, soft songs of love in their ears. Stirring

desire, that one was told to repress. Lulled to their fate,
to be mothers, fated not, to yet know physical love.

I've known only the mother that grows deep within me.
I've not known seas.

* Sita's parents were King Janaka of Mithila and Sunayana; Mary's parents were Joachim and Anna. Sita had two sons; Mary had one.

# Sita In Her Exile

It may pay to make sense of the scene:
As the sun blankets the moon, its spreading paint,
writing flaws into the moon's bones, he gazes at her
with devotion deep in the forest where, sinking their feet
together, she returns to him the look of a Prometheus.
The stare does not suggest boundaries.

The peacocks hiss in wild ecstasy,
their notes quick gutting the forest's sly silence.
Doubling, then reversing, *peehaw*, *peehuu*, they screech.
Their rumors drive the golden deer crazy.
Their tails spread wide, as they would burn down
the glory of the trusted sun. Like the *madira* of their
long tails dragging, then suggesting, operatic masks,
their ruling crowns tilt, recklessly like petals, as it were.

There is a strange desire chanting, a golden mask
shakes the bough of longing. She rides on it,
then asks him for a golden deer. As children plead,
possession possessed her, plucked to the core. The lord
of rebellion wears a cleft crown. So her husband lays down,
a fine line drawn in white around her cottage. She insists,
the fruit would fall to the ground, but she would not touch.

Meanwhile, the train of peacocks does not relent.
Their crowned heads bob in relentless self-esteem.
They walk on the aroma of myrrh, a mesh of white liquid
blurring the sunken line, its powdered remains on which,
a lone peahen reaps a tear; it rolls down her cheek, then
becomes smug, begin its molting in degrees of comfort.

And yet she seems happy, in the throes of her *agni-pariksha.* *
Like an artist, in perfect alignment with her chronicled exile.

---

* Sita's trial by fire.

## Sita's Red Riding Hood

The kind of grand daughter who delights in enticements;
whose delectation is the sight of the cunning wolf.
He says, enthused, "I want to see your grandmother just once.
When she's right inside me." At which, in disbelief,
we wonder why he didn't gobble her up right there,
cluck surreptitiously, cough into her fable's silly truths.

The mother isn't amused at such inherent negligence
that has brought down kingdoms, much less little red caps,
like crossing a sanctified line. Still, no one knows quite
what to do with so much blushing innocence.
On occasion their names have been brought up
before the courts of fairytale law. They wait,
like all innocent lasses do for the wicked stranger.
For the forest is virginal, its green flashing forth
the rhythms of desire, to scalp the offending leaves.
Some trailing drops of red left, tearful pickings,
like anonymous warnings in a sad peeling away.

Yet the monk goes on like some protective Pan,
a lord of the forest (all of it the subtle kind),
for whom no *Lakshman Rekha* exists, no boundary
too sharp to be embraced, no magic potion too fine
to rest in his saffron garb, unknown, unseen. Grimly,

promising marvels to those who would betoken charity.
When last she was seen, she seemed to wear
a mocking grimace, for some of us who try to
claim divine understanding, seek propitiation,
even notes from the dead, ask about her, where
she might have gone after leaving the wolf's stomach,
a former life that might explain presages, the silences
that startle, the odd confusion of prowling in a forest,
nor tipping the dead thought about one's naiveté,
boxed in a hut. The beast, they say, could fashion well.

So, thus so, many Sitas risk their red riding hoods,
And the wolf continues to lurk in the forest.

* Both Sita and the young girl in the Red Riding Hood fairytale were warned against lurking danger in the forest. Sita was asked never to cross the boundary line of her hut.

# Durga Power

1

When the black mantle of Mahisa held sway,
and all was but darkness and death around,
from knowledge of ourselves we lost the way,
swifter than the demon, she beat to the ground.

With awesome might, her lion charioted by desire,
to prove his undying devotion and his love,
and at her feet and like her son, to draw his fire
grappled with the demon that she held from above.

But his wicked heart flaming with brute unrest,
Mahisa hit the earth with his gigantic tail,
dispersed the clouds from heaven's pink breast,
and emptied the oceans through his bitter rail.

Immortal his might when no man could him kill,
that boon the gods gave him made him vain,
dodging and hiding as a buffalo shape until,
a woman with a thousand arms drove him insane.

He hissed and hurled tall mountains about,
for destruction was a puny leviathan's art,

his hooves and his horns were his evil route,
until she pulled her trident through his heart.

As the red stream of blood gushed out, in wonder
the gods stopped, gazing again at the tongue they'd seen.
It darted and flicked about, like Shiva's subtle thunder
miming the *tandava* in twilight's fading beam.

Like as her mother goddess counterparts that be,
like as their radiance, dissolving into a merciful smile,
infinite Jagadamba grace of Uma, Ambika, Kali, Parvati,
nurture a spiritual energy, unbeknown becomes her bile.

2

Returning to celebrate her energy in a yearly votive,
we strum to the sounds of *dhaak*, the exalted charm
of new woven silks, the gaily spun *pandals* festive,
the *shiuli* thrilling the soft diaphanous air of all harm.

The lotus lighting the seven centers of her body in bliss,
the racing joy of *kaash*, her *kundalini* and the holidays
strung like nine pearls on a watchful neck, the cloying kiss
of sweets, or an occasional animal sacrifice like a disgrace.

The elephants elegantly caparisoned, the streets aflush,
with eager faces, lonely, lovely, the loveless and the loved,
caressing her ten arms, bow and arrow agog, the spear refreshed,
her conch and discuss, rosary, bell, a wine cup, shield and sword.

And then her image with that gorgeous long hair borne,
luxuriant in royal red flair, those luminous eyes supreme,

reflecting her will, and those rare tinsel ornaments adorn,
sunk into the gullet of the waters as it would seem.

Pausing, reflecting, on the strength of one beyond reach,
the celebration of an annual rite, those drops of femininity,
untouched by a husband-god, neither depend nor beseech,
we wander, pilgrim-like, wonder about psychic totality.

When night cast its wings on the wetness of this earth,
when the tassels of the river promised to run its course,
when the wind disturbed its gut with a reckless mirth,
then the sacred fires burned steadily and with slow force.

The sun shone wearily amid its resplendent tatters,
then the departing goddess, a boon from his golden heart,
suckle, nourish, vegetation grow from her molding matter,
vanished as she promised to play her *Sakambhari* part.

---

* Through her heroic exploits, Durga reverses and even violates the model of a Hindu woman in her submissive role. Mahisa, a demon, who had a boon never to be killed by a man, was eventually destroyed by Durga.

# The Blackness of Kaali

I thought that all the colors blend, in the muddling, merging
of her blackness. Until she escapes between its sharpened teeth.

I thought that her ruddy tongue protrudes, drunk with insult,
hot with a mixed message for lolling evidence of manhood.

I thought that she wears a necklace of skulls, inherited from
a world that hires her to sweep the meat scraps from her body.

I thought that her clothing is a girdle made of dead men's hands,
for those have pushed and shoved the crook of her bare bosom.

I thought that her three eyes bloodshot, wait to finish the tale
half-told, those feasting on the exaggerations of her broken crotch.

I thought that her face besmeared with blood, is a naked parade,
the overheard cries of shame, being raped again and yet again.

I thought that her four arms, demon in one, sword in the other.
And none to singe, macerated crowds of her own ill-borne womb.

I thought that she likes to stand with one foot on the thigh, the other
on the breast of her husband luring her in a sideshow shadow.

I thought that she wears nothing in order to hide herself conjured,
by her own creations, the one and only bodily truth, her blackness.

I thought that her hair hangs loose, for the world looks shiny,
entangled in the knots of her subdued sobs of despair.

I thought that she likes to live near the dead, seeking
signs of vitality, dissolving, squeezing, those near, vapors.

I thought that she likes to dance, in fevered pitch nourishing,
her wild hope for a patch of the dead earth, a wily wilderness.

I thought that she likes the black blood to be let; huddled in her,
is the breath knocked free, the monthly fires of a bleeding woman.

---

* Kaali is the goddess of wrath and vengeance. She represents primeval *shakti* or strength.

## To Lakshmi

There are two kinds of women, rich and poor,
and you always remind me of another kind.

Now, one stands on a full-blooming lotus,
and the other falls on its anti-obvious muck.

While gold coins cascade from the side of one,
the other smiles, missing the mark of mimesis.

Even though one wears a gleaming red and gold,
the other rubs her ruby cramps with her loincloth.

It's not that the two elephants would spray for nothing,
for the other sinks under the silver weight of sorrow.

Every time she raises two of her four dainty hands,
the other drops a sigh, her hands in rhythmic melting.

Warm walls close around one in her womenistic bliss,
the doorknobs rot, recalling the other's domestic deity.

How many women would prosper by their namesake?
While the other loses, even the sound of her sanity.

There is no art in her divine beauty that spreads,
though how would you chart the rays of the other?

The success that you thought was material, is not,
while the other swears that it is irreplaceable.

There are two kinds of women, poor and rich,
and you always remind me of another kind.

* Lakshmi is the Hindu goddess of wealth and prosperity.

## Draupadi's Angst

Her copper-skinned body surging, anonymous, an ocean,
wraps five husbands, sealed in fortune's slick wheel.

Her granite will counters enemies, tosses them like fireflies,
rubs them in her princess's palms that wouldn't tip or slant.

Follow her father's curse; he wouldn't share, and she must,
the oracle's sufficiency is but a parade of her presence.

Full grown the proud geography of her pervasive being,
she sprung from the womb of a fire that would breathe.

Feminine desire is but a bitter thing; she must regenerate it,
in several stances of feeling that cancels out self-definition.

Charmed by one who must shoot into the arc, proud, unbending,
she must hold him in her lustrous lair but once every fifth year.

Or else share him with others; this misplacement of conjugality
is a cruel thing, omitting all traces of proud burning stars.

Women lusting for other husbands, casually bond, her victim
self, strongly weakened, then fall from a frosty heaven.

Common as chattel, pledged in a game of dice, crying, snarling, mock bitter oaths, turning painter-like, upon their own ferocity.

Dragging those fabulous tresses, disrobed by that besieging pain, the nudity of Draupadi's unending fabric, conceals her no less.

* In the epic poem, *Mahabharata*, Draupadi, the daughter of Drupad, the king of Panchala, is the wife of the five great Pandavas. Her cruel fate divides her as a possession among five husbands and cuts up her personality.

## Mira Bai's Aubade

When morning comes, dense with your peerless love,
I wonder where love has disappeared in the modern world.

Milkmaids churning the curd, with the jangle of bangles,
I wonder then, what love could mean in the modern world.

When cowherds wait for my lord, Girdhar, and the sound
of your flute cleanses souls, I wonder why it needs cleansing.

What does it mean that the morning has arrived, devotes
itself, each house opens its doors to the sound of my songs.

They say that I threw away my pride to be with you,
I wonder then, what if my husband had not been killed?

Had he been devoted to my dark lord as much as I am,
would I not practice his suspicions, or gladly fall in love?

When I call myself your servant, women wonder why
I would slave and serve a lord I cannot see nor touch.

Begging bowl in one hand, my cymbals in the other,
is it not easier to drink the venom of others' malice?

My orange tatters show the arrow has pierced my heart,
I'd rather sing my songs of *bhakti* than be tossed around.

Dancing barefoot with the lowly ones is an art,
I'd rather lose my self than suit your convenient need.

If my love is romantic, and if your flute drives me crazy,
I wonder why my love is invoked and then revoked?

If I still love to worship you, along with a bunch of silly *gopis*,
why do other young girls think I am only good for poetry?

But that I would prefer to be powerless in your love,
this is a question that begs another question.

---

* Mira Bai is a legendary devotee of Krishna.

## Parvati's Penance

Daughter of the king of mountains, you would but persevere,
though your mother, a bundle of chagrin and exasperation,
stopped you from your penance, your meditation, and
your unchanging posture, a delight, for you finally won.
How many women yearn to be like you, desire, your desire?

His first love now dead, Shiva buried himself in his dark sorrow.
The earth was a tomb, ageless as his distraught silence. His *tapas*
a performance, resplendent, energy bursting, brutally empty.
And so you resolved to coil around him. Wean energy from him,
do good to the world, desperate for his semen, father your child.

You reincarnate yourself, a woman born anew, with *shakti*
that made you, royal-born, sweep his floor, offer him fruits,
look upon him with so much love longing, adorn his dull cavern
with blossoms. Those goddesses you invoke, that pleasure garden
where you lustily aim, at him, drip fragrance, the bees buzzing.

Alarmed, his third eye blinking, such rage is not good for a god,
reduce, the flames gather wind, *kama* dies and is reborn a maiden;
win the heart of the ascetic, sail on pollen's wings. Winning
him is like ruling him, barren world decadent in abundance,
you hunt, you yield, turn over the pale tissue of innocence.

Of married felicity such a loud trumpeter, it seems uncanny
to prove it a fertile rite. But your penance waits for the road,
less set forth in its ways, less a burden than a triumph; to seek
the long life of a husband is fine, though less intense,
than the distribution of its finer, its shinier properties.

---

* Parvati, the other half of Shiva, symbolizes virtues esteemed by Hindu tradition: fertility, marital felicity and devotion to the spouse. She is especially worshipped by married ladies who seek the health and longevity of their husbands.

# Amba's *Swayamwara*

The truths were born, more than three thousand years ago.
They were born before she met him at her *swayamwara*.

And so when those daughters grew young, they would be
given away. And the king, their father, would have it so.

That gold-tinsled hour arrived; the suitors came in parallel glory
a contest the king set up for Amba, Ambika, Ambalika.

Two of the king's pretty daughters were but wise, marrying
from the contenders, young men with skills and charms.

Amba, charmed to a slow chase, insisted on marrying a youth
who said he could never marry; staying lucent in his singleness.

She gave her heart to one who refused her a thousand times;
enraged, she swore to kill him, at least in her next life, or die.

The wheat fell from the stalk; the birds stopped their songs.
The war raged on, and Amba withered away single, sad, singular.

And so Amba's *swayamwara* came to naught her garland crushed
in incremental fallouts, like the weight of their doubtful petals.

Like the weight of her walking stick, long dropping hours of life,
the bottom of commerce, and the watchful confrontation again.

Desperate, dulled, dried of tearful demands, she would not deny,
only demand his hand in marriage, the *swayamwara* denied her.

Only when *Shikhandi* was born, she sought her luminous revenge
the man who refused to marry her, impotent warrior scabbed.

The anger of the weak never goes away; only, it gets a little moldy.
But the shared and the sharing of strength gets weakened thereby.

---

* In the *Mahabharata*, Amba is rejected by Bhishama who has vowed to be an eternal bachelor. Amba is instrumental in Bhishama's death when she is reborn as Shikhandi.

## *Ganga Maiyya* or Mother Goddess

Let tenderness be an art. Mothers don't need to learn it.
But they must perfect it. Telling the truth about so-called joys
must be painful. The pain frames me in its shock tactics.

Son, do you know it instinctually when I feel lonely?
May be you should. I wish you would. I crave for your
understanding. And I keep waiting for a show of that love,
that never comes back. To that time when you were free,
to come into my arms, to let me hold you so tight, it hurt you so.
It frightened you to know that the storm bursting in my heart
would never abate. But other arms grip you now.
Since you have entered another woman's womb, other arms
frame you, and I fret that you have relinquished your freedom
that was so much a part of me once.

Let the artist explore. In exhaustive searches for the wounds,
of love, and of bitter conquest. She does so much that she has
a little of her own left with her, plods to her bittersweet grave.

Child, do you understand me when I feel tired? Maybe you do.
Why is my resentment staring me in your face? Or,
is it yours? Is your love a partial secret? Why must my pain
be so murderous to you when you grow up? I was told that
a woman and a mother must go hand in hand. And yet I find

my hands untie the lust of love's boredom. You thrust in me, bone upon bone. It frustrates me endlessly, and I dab my blind tears with unattended joy. I chase my memories of you. They still come home to roost. I feel dirty; you hand me more dirt. This dirt would fascinate me otherwise, but for now,

I dream of a motherless paradise.

* The sacred river, Ganga, is revered as a mother.

## Gandhari's Blindfolded Life

Her eyes, so now she has sealed them off, see
what her husband must see among the caverns
studiously unavailable. For him, she wanders among
vast rooms that are sensuous shades, cinema palaces
where she can let loose her restricted guise, and
assume another. And still she claims happiness.

Noble wife indeed, to shrink from the arms that
she could see and then embrace them with fire gold.
Sealed across those dim holes that can only destroy
the erotic violence of this naked world. She would
but deny herself those nameless flowers that she dare
tread, though she knew them in her slitted non-light.

Wise woman indeed, to claim a kind of protection
from the wily luxuries that he could scrape through
and that would trouble her more, than the few jabs of
hate that cut through genes and blood, commingled.
With ire that turns the axis of victory to those who
can only kill, for bloody roots of a laurelled-head.

Her eyes, so that they may never weep, rest unused.
To the redundant wants that clog the will, the stops
that pull at philosophy's footsteps, that make metric

advances toward the floodlights. Until they dim, and
grow used to their own disuse. Then she places it aside,
watching glumly at the passing parade, this naked world.

* Gandhari, wife of Dhritarashtra in the Indian epic, *Mahabharata,* was married to a blind man. She thought she should not enjoy any luxuries of life that were denied to the husband, and so she blinded herself with a cloth.

# Urmila's Protest

Why would you pity me or even remember my unknown fate?
What does it matter to be tied to a husband as to hell's gate?
For marrying a man of Lakshmana's size would be a torrent roar,
whether we lived the marriage bubble fourteen years less, or more.

Why would you have me share my sister's lot through the forest?
What did she get for her undying devotion at her husband's behest?
For living amid peculiar beasts and wild cacti their stingy nape,
is no fun when we can be free, unbound in single women's shape.

Why is my husband's or my sister's fate more glorious than mine?
What do I care for a silly feminist's wail, a leftist bleacher's whine?
I lived life without a promp, he choked in his brother's loyal dust.

Why should happiness come to those who are husband bound?
What then remains after women have plied their domestic trade?
Unfit to love or be loved, by then beyond all domestic peace,
afflict with galls and sores, flutter menopausal wings ere decease.

Why should you assume what you would, in my lonely state?
What worse than to hover, seethe in the thralldom of my mate?
Lest we think that women's oppression is a storyteller's tale,
invincible, ungleaming, without history's moan or bitter rail.

---

* Urmila, wife of Rama's younger brother, Lakshmana, remains unknown to history.

# The Texture of Devaki's life

That woman who drives into town seeking fertility treatment,
tries out *Clomiphene citrate*; it flows through her, then her face
fades, as she knows she would ask for more potent means, for the
vision of children in green ink; the backyard play toys titter.
She needs as much assurance as that which made Devaki a queen.

*Human Menopausal Gonadotrophin* promises her grander success
mix hormones, push her ovaries to make eggs that catch wings,
with no side effects. Because that infant tugs at her warm breast,
ovulate with extra delight, like that which smeared Devaki with
a son's smell, the soil bare now, weed out, smudge, trod over.

Remarkably, her ovaries hyperstimulate, leak anger all over.
She screams, refuses challenge, as if challenge is a grand lord
dismounted once awhile, spear in hand, curse all the newborn.
And Devaki must seem demented, obtusely so, as she ejects child
after child from her tireless womb; she looks on, languish on
the soft spot of a vision, terrible and total, like a stranded chill.

While she continues to look on, stone in hand to rouse her fate,
Devaki's womb spills and gushes the eighth time over as if locked
in sexual disgust, so that the egg is hatched without the sperm,
withstood its own in barren ones, and a baby god jumps out,

flute in hand, promising help to her, while the sky looms large in her frame of gathering, as if to explain the fertility difference.

---

* In Hindu mythology, Devaki, the wife of Vasudeva and mother of Krishna was feared by her cousin, Kamsa, due to a prophecy that one of their sons would kill him.

## Kunti's Secret Mantra

Well, it would be nice to bear a child by a god, I told her.
She smiled and nodded, almost as if she would confer it on me.
And so her gift came to pass. Her five sons tumbled out, while
her husband longed for another. She yearned for his touch, while
he passed on. A gaze so full of broken earnestness, it made her.

Fall apart in a surface wound like situation. She mirrored nothing,
but the self. With a smile that any man would die for, she groped
for secular satisfaction, that resembled intense poetry sessions, the
kind that made her sons drive heat in their innards, seek war glory
against the ethics of resentment. She assigned them no triviality

Only plugged into them a life running on the fuel of conscience.
So much so that the oldest willed himself to share his booty with
his brothers, cloning her desire. Singing and rejoicing on summer
nights, she asked herself. What could be worse than her own fate,
stirred. Or that to be shared with hers. She reckoned with this.

Foolish piece of rejected news, I balked, drooled in silly jealousy,
as if the experience was with the god, and not the mantra that tied
her to her womb. Wherein lie my eyes that seal affection as gather
wit. In clever circles of denial, then lighting a match to my seal.
Almost as if they too touched me. By her secret mantra.

---

* In the *Mahabharata*, Kunti, mother of the *Pandavas,* had a boon to be blessed with a child by any god.

## Duty-Bound Uma

That time he nailed himself up once again, almost without forewarning,
like a sultan stretching himself in his kitchen floor of a harem, she came
back to him, wrenching her hands tight over his eyes, playing with him as
with her dolls in bad weather. He clenched her wrist tight in wrinkled anger.
Her fear brimming, a ripe secret, she begged forgiveness, like one entranced.

Unused to such episodes, she stood enchanted, while he blazed, shaking her up.
Knocking her down, swinging his mood left and right, knocking up her dolls
that came in his mighty path. Then storming out of her door, all ablaze, a meadow
full of bright yellow flowers. She ran after him, threw herself at her lord's feet,
rubbing her dainty head on the hardened floor, bubbling from inside, tears and all.

She felt something wither, an old woman with a haunted look, it cracked forever

while she pledged to herself to disavow self-indulgence. Smiling
gladly, benignly,
stolid with conviction, forbearance watched her light arrive, even
as her heart wept,
only so she could become duty-bound? Only so she could by her
own ruse be deigned,
a construct, of self-sacrifice? Of clever submission, for it could be
nothing else.

How she fooled her own mother with the glimmering
annunciatory plan,
who cried out in gleaming pride, 'U!Ma!' She quietly left for the
psychiatrist,
who pronounced the verdict of clinical depression, handed her
complimentary pills,
asked her if she cried naturally? Naturally, she replied. Proud to
have glory reaped
upon her wifely self; he played his regal portion, whispered into
the dove's ears.

Then sprang into full form, Shiva-like, saw the tears run out, the
sourly parted
waters. Until the facts of married life bloat up, ugly, dangling,
disabused cargo.

* Uma is one aspect of the great Goddess of Indian mythology known as Devi ("the goddess"). Even as her husband frequently ignored her, she practiced harsh self-denial.

## Bhairavi the Terrible

Crimson stones and wild suns grow amuck on her,
and yet she remains fine-veined, smiling, silken veil ribbed
in pink, the blood on her breast hangs on with bright red scars
thrown back against lotus-faced shadows, debunking ignorance.
Scarlet features tumble down her tall, valorous steps
screaming transcendent knowledge, as if it were
so much within our reach, it would thrust through,
and her diadem brushes the moon's silver tiles.
On a black lacquered table she sits, inherently shining.
For death begins from the very moment of birth.

Smooth as her death-drenched beads, lust-ridden.
The fearful servant stretches her hand into history
and just as the wind whispers the story of destruction
she turns to wear a garland of skulls. Many senses stir,
her shapely figure conceals the elusive thread of desire,
bewitched fruit, intoxicating, caressing, almost tantalizing,
the *shakta-pramod** form, worship the semen of sexual life.
And a stray memory drifts through the abyss, breathless,
splintered, evocative, almost like god's silence on this earth,
for death is present in almost all of our nakedly physical beings.

Another weak-limbed tree dapples the damp ground,
preconceived ideas grow, flourish, like soft-pulped fruit

governed by the rind of illusions, unseen in the darkness,
waiting for those who gather the juice, that bewitched fruit
with gnarled fingers, touch pulls, close eyes, spell-bound laughter,
dreaming, screaming, slithering, down the alleys of foreboding,
hoarse cries of expectation resound, struggling to conceive spells,
consumed with rinsed wrath, procreating, dissolve the eternal eye
of cosmic conception, the formless waters part, a scrap of intuition,
for freedom begins in freedom from that thinned bondage.

---

* Bhairavi has multiple facets and manifestations that reinforce the Hindu goddess's cosmic importance and supremacy. One commentary suggests that the name Bhairavi is derived from the words *bharana* (to create), *ramana* (to protect) and *vamana* (to emit or disgorge). Hence, the inner meaning of Bhairavi's name can be identified with the cosmic functions of creation, maintenance and destruction.

# Almost Two Sinners, Shabari and Mary Magdalene

At one point, Shabari fell at his feet, this lonely lowly woman.
At one point, he picked her up and rocked her to his heart.

Then she bared her bosom, only so much that Mary's thick red hair
could not conceal. He gripped her, then grappled, then turned.

Shabari vowed to risk her true intent. Dense with *bhakti* longing,
she cast herself adrift, sonorous as a birdsong, split the seed.

They decided to stone this Mary wretch to death, her apparent
profanity had touched them so, blend their venom with desire.

But Shabari pleaded with so much comprehension, such liquid
like humbleness, it seemed profane to be so devout, suffer so.

Then Mary turned to penance, soothing as death, wash the feet,
and the village banter, of another wretch, leper-like his designs.

And Shabari pitied her so, bled for her in tears rank as mud pile
soaked in sapless leaves, veins twisted, as eggs of red gleaming.

That awakening came to them in falling measures, seek the lock
and key in the low places where sinners rejoice hymn-like poses.

Tortured, surreal as their poetry, they found it in sinning together, for sinning comes slow, between a light conscience and solid gold.

Sparing them, then faulting along fine fault lines. Forgiveness is an open marriage that stumbles into discoveries, healing, then not.

* Shabari and Mary Magdalene have both been reviled and honored in the Hindu and Christian traditions.

## Mandodhari's Grief

She smiles, tilted mouth, happy as a bee, buzzing abuzz
with hands cupped, purring, when the mischievous glare
of that long afternoon makes her feel tall, aglow, the leaves
blossom in their new art, the rain, pouring, then succumbs.

Only in that happy meantime, she has not let up, with wicked
straggly peace, the rhythms of richness, stretch, her eyes open,
observers blend in with the extraordinary struggle of the prime,
of life, her simplicity catching waves, nor unmistakably in triumph.

Between the sunless dawn and the windy wind, the gossip
hounds pronounce her stuck, see no soft stones in her pockets,
no amber traps here, no storms in her life, nor does she ask herself
whither profits, until the sun feels corrupted with the soggy weeds.

Explode the sleeping face of laughter, nor pretend, for self-knowledge
is an art. With puckered lips, waves to all her friends, nor does she
sabotage desire. Neat rows forward-thinking, meticulous as matter,
arches her eyebrows, brave chaste bosom, swelling, a soft blur.

Give up the ghosts, the shadow monk in saffron robes, disrobing
the white circumference of one married. Props an arm on her side,
giggle at silly jokes in her pitched empire, luxury-strength, clip
the lotuses that wallow, stench-filled, with wondrous glazed eyes.

She dreams, an island kingdom filled with love, the waters drown the thread that links her to honorable earth, strings memories of a departed age, warm-blooded, nor ready to snap, less unforgiving, smiles, laps tiny lights, ten shades touching her forehead, in a gentle current.

---

* Mandodhari is wife of the demon king of Lanka, Ravana, who desired and abducted Sita.

## Is Shurpanakha a Dalit Woman?

What hands are those that strike us down,
then rip us open, like the wound of love going home?

When women propose, with their big brawny hands,
why would men strike down our desire, cut a nose or a leg?

What men are those that scar us with their name-calling,
bruise or bare our bosoms, force us to eat that wisp of a cloud?

When a woman's knee joint splinters, the sound loud as the crack,
why would that taste of the semen that was once her safety net?

What whip is that which soothes and charms both together,
frames us in its implications, then releases as a hardened spring?

When we dare, why be blamed for the exuberance of wars,
When all the blood-consuming is but a close plan to insinuate?

What shame is that which disables every worthy cause, to resist,
remembers vengeance like the flashing sea and the dark rain?

When we turn into victims, our fate sorrowed like bumpy hills,
why would survival seem a paper-thin veneer of full slanted life?

What seed is that lodges in the gold dust of winter afternoons, then brims with hideous laughter, like a prince's abusive charms?

When the trees blow on a dead-still day, turn the dead corner,
why do we see the trees whir, stray bullets sprayed between them?

---

* Shrupanakha is Ravana's sister. She desires Rama and is said to have acted in revenge after she is humiliated. She is thereby reckoned to have started the epic war.

## Rohini the Favorite

They both dance, and while he trails behind her,
hers is a comic dance, a kind of puppetry, a stealthy
winning over; the grayness parting the waters for him.

Every day he goes in search of her, forsaking
his pride, the spherical pavement on which he would,
fling his bobbin, nibbling on crumbs as he would her pearls.

Then she would extricate herself from his grasp,
sighing for her father and singing in the same breath,
happy as the first light of summer, a proper distance though.

He touches her slender foot, and she trembles,
catching her breath, pulling, until he whirls as though,
her witchery would send them both into exile.

The rest of them fake even the question mark,
scorched within, dead from the sharp twist of his knife,
catch their breath, and laugh as though he were in their arms.

They practice their monthly trade with aplomb,
accommodate the generations of wombs before and after,
while he chants his literature of love in the same cycle.

But when the singing becomes incessant, they wail,
and when her father cursed his luminous falsehood, he agreed,
so all of them dance with him, one by one, in eloquent gestures.

Quite leisurely though, and with breathless slings,
he chases her alone, month after month, sublime love
turns his coral head aglow, glistens, full blown, at violent ease.

And yet there is a calamity, when he stares at her one lone night
of every single month, resplendent in her loneliness, mocking,
as if he were nothing but a reflection of her.

* In one version of Hindu mythology, Rohini is said to have been the favorite of the twenty-eight wives of the moon.

## Kausalya, The Co-Wife

She prepares fresh *chapattis* every morning, but the smell
of burned sugar still haunts her. An empty doorway, and steps
leading up to her bedroom, the lights above dipping and hissing.

Her penchant for submission, like watercolor submitting to
its own ink. The songs of beggars echoing off the sugar-smell,
burned through the blade of self-denial, until she leans yet further.

She presses her head against the palette of light descending,
and its texture approaches the shape of her sisters' heels clicking,
of lovemaking with her maker, then she gives birth to him.

She hears voices, bears witness to the elegant language of joy,
and everyday he shuts her up, slabs of sugar echo soft pink black,
reacts trendily, forsakes tongue, forsaking the romance of fashion.

He struts down every morning, mornings filled with stored suns,
useless to her, her sisters lying in darkness, sunlight spills on her,
tortured *chapattis* tell a story, in small letters, as the smell escapes.

She dreams of a political plan until the smell chokes her,
birth beauty-determined, she withdraws into her deliberate dream
in the voice of that she had lacked, traditional tunes of silence.

While history waits for her, the sizzle of motherhood in hand,
like an underground train, she inhales exhaust from the streets,
her dazed smile delicate in its tough recognition of her honor.

---

* Kausalya was one of three wives of Rama's father. She was also Rama's biological mother.

## Annapurna's Food Fixation

*Rasgullas* in the middle of the night, wonder
why she steals them in the name of a gentle god;
this mindless ballooning up is a lie, like smoking
with a friend on a warm windless night, then letting it
all pile up within, all his words, contaminated, food-like.

As if what he said to her yesterday can reflect on itself,
while he throttles her with his wonder talk, idiot wife, smelling
like larceny, no one could sit next to her, so she leaves
his room, swapping emptiness in exact proportions,
and believes that being overweight is a deft construction.

Once in cold weather, when her hand split on his
hardened knuckles, she went on the loose, ate out of fear,
ate out of love, ate out of meaning, ate with none, ate because,
her fear, razed to the ground, she found herself making
a perfect circle, all his songs sung in cordial unison.

She spat at paranoia, that a man like him could be tall,
over and over, thus spoken, sizing her ninety-three kilos
his look, condescension softly overflowing, tells his tale,
"Who wants your ugly body?" acts like a humble thief,
"Why don't you go back to your mother's house?"

Flees in self-betrayal to the refrigerator, sips green tea,
sliding gently by the glass of juice, nibbles at the *rasgullas*,
squeezes out the syrup from its haunches, green salad sits curled
on her knees, spared. He said something to her again, by the nick
of her stolen ears, she sits there in frozen agony, stuck, like herself.

* Annapurna is a Sanskrit word that literally means "complete food." The goddess Annapurna symbolizes wholesome and complete nourishment.

## Because my Great-Grandmother Refused to Become *Sati*

I hate the suggestion of a fire, for fire can only burn,
intrepid, zealous, devour the suggestion of life, beyond his.

I hate to think of volition, for self-will is demeaning,
inexcusable, wretched, yellow flames licking, lick imperiously.

Impious woman, scratching Manu's laws, flogging morality,
take it by its locks, then throw it into the hearth, bedrock rocking.

She loved to live, wanting more, life's bitter hills bumping
her up and down, thumping her plum-colored spirit, never give in.

So that yellow-haired demon had a tough warrior, rough-hewn,
tempered by the course of family life, glitter like dust, like life.

That mob threw her in, and the charcoal, their joyous parade,
yellowing sunset, she ran out, against the copper pot, his ashes.

And I hate the suggestion of another fire. I would have cold cuts,
cold food in hot weather is happier than a festive self-immolation.

The charred remains of my cold food are stuck, floating; for the

ferry carrying my great-grandmother to the dead refused to burn.
I hate the suggestion of warming myself up; the cold, bitter faces
cast *sati** shadows, my window drenched, brushed by black lips.

The fireplace stays in darkness, a virtuous shadow, as I place the
twenty cent tin cup inside, would burn, else climb high fences.

* *Sati* refers to the immolation of a widow on her husband's pyre.

## Noor Jehan's song to a *Purdah* Woman

If I were to nail my head to a cross, I would still be happy.
If I were forced to wear dark glasses all my life, I could still
cast a fiercely supreme glance at those beneath me and above,
if I were thrown wretched glances, and taken to be
the most wretched one, I would walk over it, and carve
a stiff upper lip on all things banal. I could even toss a
cigarette butt at them, and refuse to offer a quick apology.

Doubt is a word that lies, so I wear black that I see not.
When they pulled me out of my mother's womb, my wailing
notes, tipped in invention's melody, accorded with the scale.

The wings of progression are bent over by practice; so my *riyaz*
constitutes the forestalling of any rebuke. In metallic timbers
I seek the self about me, *Mallika-e-Tarranum*, more than a queen.

Three classical forms, flailing pulse, rising rhythms that I
mimic to perfection. You watch me slow my tempo, the whims
adrift in the beats of the *thumri*; for her who rose like a courtesan.
Then fell to the breeds of her trade. Then rose to perfect the art
of devotion as a futile rite. Singing *dhrupads*, love's lonely
trumpeter, in simple selective steps.

If I were to display virtuosity to the stars, I could turn to those *khayals* that would nurture my sorrow in the raw haloes of love that feels like thrombosis, it pains so much. I would scatter its words in pieces or in whole. I would close myself off in my *purdah* of remembering. Until swans disrupted my music, and matched my notes with their grace.

Love was held back by its shadow, so I had to seek communion with so many lovers. Celebrate its rites in blood drops. Then wipe my feet over it.

---

* Noor Jehan was a famous singer and film star.

## Her Survival Kit

Botox my face. A bird swoops down and picks a crumb.
The art of looking younger is to smile always.
Mask your true feelings. Endure, endure.

I will not wince nor set my teeth on edge.
No overly ambitious attempt to force my words
into a disarray. Receive the god as in a faceless throng.

Drive the flint of patience, into the soggy heart,
into the realist's mirage, forestall any further harvests,
to tint the dark fungus on the soul, a tad more.

Decorum is a thing that stands on regal heads,
so I wear last spring's plunder, spray painted
in small red letters, to call my mind there.

I live on thin and frail edges. I like to live on them.
For passing over larger clumps becomes easy, settled
in my choices, like an aged, crummy highway overpass.

I only let my mother know, and when she throws darts,
at me, her preferred quarry, I slither down her neck,
and stain her bloodless womb once again.

I try not to commit errors, for then I have to scrub
so much that all of my soul hurts with the effort.
I scrub and scrub, and then explode. Wetness spills.

On my calm face, like an alchemist's golden charm.
Survival is thought to be a technique, like ratcheting up
your score on this earth's bitterly hungry dugs.

## Upon Sighting the Moon

That midnight moment when she awoke
and saw the full moon hanging as a picture
in between the drapes that framed her window,
the dove descending from the sky, fluttered, paused.

She fell in love with him, for her tears, mystical, strung
in an absolute act, braided, incandescent.
She could not but weep, a maiden affrighted,
she vowed to throw water at its crested sight.

Do not weep, sister, for love is an unexplained art,
turning its selections like a sieve, crying hoarse to
the hungry soul that was born to fly or die,
without being shriven.

When graded needles, in an unforeseen pattern,
ripped her husband's body apart, she vowed
to fast from dawn's gold fingers until the pale
sunken light of that moon, teasing, cajoled.

By mild elimination of its own image, reappeared.
Swift circling its annual ritual, its subjective nature
humbled by devotion of so many married, so many
touching their husbands' feet in ritual redundancies.

Those unmarried, excluded, divorced, widowed,
those long suffering, lifting the self-styled image.
Women whose hearts hung splendid on their sleeves,
amid the palpitation of the moon, remembered.

Amid pauses, in the pomp of red veils, applauding,
their bangles clanging, graceful like the green earth.
Hewn in pots of love, bobbing in passionate embrace,
the gaze of the full moon, between drapes, estranged.

She nudged him, his sleep passing through a storm,
as her shampooed locks luxuriant fell, and the moon
its crest denuded, paused, urging him to love her forever.
Perhaps. And then the moon intruded.

---

* This poem refers to the Indian festival of *Karva Chauth,* when women fast and pray for the long lives of their husbands.

## Her Desires, The Desiring Woman

When I gather my bones, I know I am plucking them
from the supine waters of that which spewed white lava;
when I touch my lava, I know I am edging toward dust;
when I sense my dust, I know I am aquiver;
when I smell his flesh with mine, his breath touches mine,
then oozes the last of white lava.

It is a new heaven, though it is not a new earth.
My breasts stiffen, the rivers within gnash,
the moistened angel bursts open, aching to enfold.
To seize, to caress, to receive, to spill, to catapult forth.
The flushed bones ache; the sea widens to engulf.
A gasp. Then nothing. How paltry is the effort.
It dies. Or flies.

Like my exiled king uncrowned, giving away
a kingdom only worth a few paltry pennies.
I contain his rage with mine. Mine carries several
shades of desire. To lick, to lip, to limn, to lisp,
to love, to litter, to lilt, to lie down in a lull.
When the waters glitter down him to awaken me,
I sink with delight on that fine point of dust,
and the old earth shakes again.

For every woman who wants to be me.
Do I then bow at the altar of my desire?

## Did She Eat A Bite Of Eve's Apple?

And so he stirred the boiling liquid in the cauldron.
He kept stirring until that wretched stirrer disappeared.

Akin to its metaphysical pounding, its clear expansion,
does he know anything else but that she would?

Less ideally, she gets the spiritual truth from another woman,
if not from another man, though would not dare acknowledge.

The choices, he tells her, are either bewildering or,
they are intoxicating. And yet she finds none to contend with.

He rants that women are rare or rank, sluttish or disposable.
He would judge her harshly, as he would a somberly warm day.

Self-regret is like a hand-tied knot; its clumsy effort
wrapped in discreet, though impossible claims.

Respectability in a relationship does not matter,
for her, there are no savagely pressed apologies.

Some admit that they use men for their own needs,
as if need is a big white shining Rolls Royce

Is there a cloying aroma she smells?
Somewhat cloying?
Of piety?

Sniff....

He is tribe-raised, so he continues to stir, with his hands now, hand to hand, even as the apple fell from the tree, into his grip.

## Tell me, how was it sleeping with him, your real man?

Vampire woman, so would you charge me. I am vampire woman,
and I have my bulbous scars to show you what it is to be so.

"Tell me, how was the comparison? Was he hard and strong against
your suppleness? Did he satisfy you more than you willed yourself?"

I sat by his side and sucked the blood from his calf muscles.
I cannot be a means, when I am only an end, to suck myself dry.

The door swung open, and then he carried the hard, vacant look.
A relegated corpse draws his fingers across my face's fine potential.

His bloodline I would smash to smithereens, like a caulked wall.
If I had not helped him slip out of his pants, like a raven in love.

Into that tepid world of darkness, we plunge, an orgy of blood,
gut his third sight, reckless like a wounded lark, pang of death.

While my legal husband is an image-sealing saint, I am borne
on the folds of wicked breeding; screen me for generations then.

That forsaken world rests weak, into the repetitious hands of
in-breeding, the armory of charges reaps coquettes, bestial.

Three shades of night then arrive. Blasphemies perpetuated.
The ecstatic sweat burned forever, flattering nicknames for me.

# She Does Not Play With A Barbie Doll

I have learned not to play with a Barbie doll,
her face lashed by rain, the water dripping from her limp nose,
the strict shape until the dying of time and the body type,
the wheels of Mattel churning and turning,
the five feet by nine is a gigantic sprawl of a wave,
and the 36-18-33 type accuses me like a stray ripple.

All infinite things shake my finitude.
Those narrow hips are like an unread message
tossing a sliver of sunshine before it disappears,
sunk under thin folds; that concave stomach,
the sunken branch of a tree, winding around the weight
of this world, too anorexic for its heaviness.
Those pink plastic hair curlers will not curl me,
for I am a lioness with a white mane.

The freshly frozen snow on my serene lap,
sunk like burdened memories on the pages of the manual;
odor of feminine standards, like driftwood on a sunken sea-slope,
a scent beloved of teen time;
silence of water above a sunken commodity.
The teen giggles of memory in one man –
a ripple widening from a single stone
embarrassed

ashamed
expectation defied.

But I do play with a doll in a coffin with satin sheets,
odor of death and jasmine; I burn the wax candles, a shrine
to a doll that died long ago. In a windowless enclosure,
I play myself out; in my fantasy, a world in my control.

*But did I say I do not care to play with my Barbie?*
*Yes I do.*

## When Savitri's Daughter must file for Divorce

When she was eleven, she heard her mother struggle and then give in to the parody.
A nightly *mantra* where *baba* performed sex upon her mother's frail, flawless body.

She wished she could tell her mother to resist, learn to say a firm "no" to *baba*.
But she acknowledged to herself that her mother should also be a good housewife.

Her mother, she quickly learned, was skilled in subordination, and would not budge.
For she would seek her *dharma* in her namesake Savitri, married to a Satyavan.

*Baba* laid all the rules, and her mother only followed them without a murmur.
She knew then why she had been named Savitri, born to save her husband's name.

When she was twenty-one, she found her own body yearned to be saved for a name.
She married the first man *baba* let her go out with; she mapped the same old myth.

What seemed at first to be tender delight, soon became her
constant sorrow,
for her husband's will sealed her in a nightly ritual, uncontested,
seldom requited.

She wished she could tell herself to resist, then gradually learned
to say a firm "no."
His will was threatened, so he gave it back to her in subtle and
unrelenting ways.

When she was thirty-one, old enough to be a mother, she asked
her husband
if they could have a baby. He looked at her with a silent sneer,
and left the room.

She realized that they had lived parallel lives, and the fault was
all her own.
She begged her husband to forgive her, for she would please his
every whim.

He told her he would not touch her any more, for she was too fat
and gross.
And her fat and gross body did not interest him nor would any
man any more.

When she was forty-one, she found it hard to believe that it was
all over.
Her marriage had broken down, and he had gone to live with
another woman.

The lawyer came and said that he was there to help her understand
divorce laws.

Uncontested divorce, he said, would save them both time and
precious money.

Too stunned to even protest, she asked what it would cost for
legal service,
for when the distance grows too wide, the silence of speech would
catch wings.

The document arrived and she signed it out of fear of just reprisal.
The courts agreed that there was no physical abuse, no mental
torture.

Some men look at her with suspicion; others consider her a western
woman.
Some women sigh a gentle nod of understanding; others would
let it go.

Resigned to her newly acquired status, she says that nothing
much has changed.
We continue to be where we were, so much for sexual liberation.

Now Savitri's daughter is fifty-one, and menopause gives her aches
and hot flashes.
And yet she continues to believe in the myth that gave her mother
her namesake.

---

* Savitri symbolizes the ideal wife in Indian mythology.

## My Indian Sappho/The Sappho in Me

I wet my dreams with bird talk, tiny, withered,
chatting with me in obsequious silence, sinister as
abandoned children, raised to dry mouths with pellets,
dark as the darkness of hell, wrung slowly out of me.

There is a certain smell that I seek, like boiled matter,
lying for months under those baseboards, where the
water level has shifted twice, even as we frantically rinse,
the pocketful of lovemaking, neck by neck, stringed asides.

A tumult grows within me, amid all this rarefied talk,
like glue being poured onto the backs of sunbathing fish,
who look like mountain girls frozen into a dance-pose, then
bit by bit, revive like petals, naked hands turned to fresh meat.

And then we yolk, or so we want, in gestures of bones,
frightened by the marrow that ejects, lavender, then yellow,
feeling one upon another, bone mass pointing cross legged,
then feeling the weight, of anthills descending only to kill.

A tongue tickles my left ear, assembles into the subject
of that memory, the soft preparations that only she knows,
will condense, sharp as the photograph's edge jutting time,
as the puzzle that I already know, watching her hairlines weep.

The frozen fish melt, thawed by so much poignance, so much
bloodletting, the pain that grapples, wearing a brown dress,
muddy, as the abandoned children, the bones, raw in needlefuls,
the preposition that escapes, ruby red pain, strength, of the puzzle.

## Repressions and Confessions

It happened a long, long time ago,
a time when she was nine; he only sixty winters more.
The naked nymph came silently to the old shepherd.
She thought he toyed with her *pyjama* strings,
opened them, a fruit in its prime, reaping time's profits,
while she helplessly looked aside.

Pinched her breasts new budding, while midwinter
lay heavy on the house like a replaced argument.
Those moss like moments in memory, an ant's load.
When he found her alone or in passing, a child's pretense,
perhaps. In the clever maze of their two bedroom house,
he lay on her tenderly, as if the choice was hers.

She ponders on its merit. A middle-aged woman's fancy,
if it was indeed incest, that dirty word mourned, across
cultural categories, culture's wasted words, printed books,
civilization's balm, or just a subtle trick.
As if eating chicken is not the same thing.

And if she did not protest, that thing with its
velvet softness sliding inside her grotesquely large vagina,
an oddly blank look as he retracts. Don't tell anyone.
People will believe you are a bad girl.

And then he played and played again.
Who, or even what, to blame if it was meant,
to be our secret. Clearly, a non-starter. It hurt.
So he draws himself apart, as if he heard mother's
voice, and sent her to wash up her naked sins.

And when she bled, along with her reddened feces,
her mother smacked her, called her a hussy,
for she had found out.

## When Sita is Beaten up Everyday

To gossip about her being beaten up is one thing,
to suggest that she could have continued to do so
is perhaps another.

Warrior woman. You do not wish to call yourself one,
though I see bruises on your cheek every day.
The color is blue and not the abundance of
red rouge.

Your bruises are the gossamer flowers
that your husband brings to you.
When he cannot sate his own desire
to load you with the fantasies you inflicted
on your dolls. A childhood that returns
when your dolls do sleep in their doll beds,
and you do not.

The alcoholic who forces your head
into the toilet pot, the drunk who kicks
the cursed child in your cursed womb,
swears until he cries himself hoarse,
the abuser who chills you with his quiet words,
and then comforts you with icepacks, the abuser
who sugarcoats his cuss-words with niceties

honed to perfection. The violent
the dangerous
the torture.

The rapist who must drill a hole, make his rapier thrusts,
puncture your breasts, cut up your vagina, unclothe your will,
disrobe you as meat for his hungry mouth, force you to
perform your notes on his proboscidian will.

Warrior woman. You are the Sita who is beaten up everyday.

## A Modern Woman's Work Strip-Tease

Blindfolded I stand,
a weighing scale in one hand
and my naked soul in the other.

*Take if off, baby!*

The new dress I wear like whipped cream
has some earth tones and some heavenly new plans
to build on, while the scarf around my bosom
is a shadow descending. Like a balancing act,
gathering, processing, and then revealing, in fillers,
my priorities, scuttle, reaffirm. And then flip.

*Pin-up girl, Thank You for Everything.*

This landscape of my modern life
is like a coastline cracked between challenges.
The paper money that is my only worth,
spits back a wide assessment plan
how to grow, to gain more expertise.

*The walk of shame.*

There is a thin layer of grease that is my weakest link.
I gyrate on the palm of my black corselet.

I dream of stripping aside all of my lonely,
my lovely talent for constant leadership, to
take a studio loop, to snuggle into my true self.

*Bound and gagged the honey girl.*

Inadequate, vulnerable, unworthy, glamor in high heels,
tease me off this hole of my sensitivities, this tightrope walk
amid my reflective practices, my ambitions, my talents, my
Body, my, body.
Practice my slow walk, my nervous beat, my funky blues.
My soul of holiness.

*Jungle Girl, Fighting Girl, Pony Girl, Go watch Bettie bounce.*

## A Small Kitchen Fire

The story of a kerosene soaked *salwar-kameez*,
the young girl left alone to burn to ashes, because the devil
wanted to teach women to earn or to submit.

Deciding to wear a pretty string of pearls
called education, that's guile for you in pint-sized neck ware.
She kept adding a pearl every year.

As if this was not enough armor,
the furniture and new gadgets seized beyond expectation,
a car jewel, preening prize of the parade.

The mother-in-law cut her down
to her guile-less size, suggesting her father was only a
junior clerk in a beat-up government shop.

Her worth cut up, she seized upon
a weapon called mute compliance, also called *sthreedhan*.
She held it tight with a flashlight in her hand.

She would not feed the extorting vulture of
their hard edged demands sung in flashing, rising rhythms
but for the cost of seeming, opinionated.

Something spiraling between deficiency
and the brutality of owing an unlimited supply of money,
like appeasing the gluttonous dowry gods.

Simulate an act of absolute obedience
bend backward, the exquisiteness of prestigious traditions
that tell them nothing new.

The prohibition acts are like leaves,
suddenly lifted in the torturous winds spiraling upward,
then falling, like fragments, her muteness.

She dreams, of happiness of another kind,
like a poisoned smell, drowning, her struggles, then deliberate,
officials condone, then dismiss, this accidental burning.

Only the mute trees left to talk,
among themselves, when they are set up for sale,
only they blaze with burning colors.

## As an Indian Spinster Would

Crabby as delight, hang like love's might,
beget no sympathy, constant by destiny's standards.

Hoary-haired, like the trimming on a new-born, cling
like the health of an ancient planet would depend on it.

Green is to experience as honor, the new arrival,
despair catches its target at a young late twenty something.

Consider the idea, almost a perished swan of anonymity,
a fear turning to stone this thirst for the creased self.

Not in shadows, but in the sweet chinks
singing religion's hymns is but the artist's sub substitute.

Upon a point of forgiving wanton thoughts,
sodden, like the alpine run-off, buzzing, then nailing.

Coloring chaste desires with her dress limp
on the chair; turn them true, patron of chitter-chatter.

Shadows rolling, neat as narration,
field fragrance as fresh as her nervously platonic rest.

Dazzlingly verdant, distinguished, seeming
slim in waist and hip, like the riot of absorbing self-control.

Severe, stern-seeming, sense beyond senses.
Charioting the solitude of a separate living, discovered.

That shopping bag of men is cut at the underbelly,
now safe as fatherly ocean, now churning, to build new empires.

Knowing that there are no clear winners is a banality,
resurfaced, recycled, ardent as larks, then filled with waiting.

Look away, then she won't, weaving her new taste,
for expanding, then contracting, this mass of old desirings.

## Anaarkali's Dance

With her dampened dragon fire of a gaze,
the worm stirred within her, the cold, clammy tug.

This commonplace nautch girl dared to lust,
she tried to find its nuances in a prince's arms.

He squeezed her elbow, the king in his supreme might,
the cold pretension of a lasting union slashed away.

But Salim loved her like a chopping and weeping idiot.
For why should not love be supreme if it is not meant to be?

Emperor, you lay down the laws of love, and then
you want us to defy them, like the rhythms of her dance.

All things become extraordinary by vanishing,
and after all, it is the fate of women to succumb.

So the king advised her to pretend, as only
a dancing girl could, to practice her posture.

An unremembering, as if she did not love Salim.
So she danced with marvelous terror, this dance of love.

The fetid smell of ditches and ponds could but relent,
gently tapping, she danced unto a deathly bitterness.

The king buried her alive; behind the walls of the bazaar,
the shadow dances, for it is better to have this nothing.

And when the over blossoming nature of her dance
becomes her predator, she pauses. Sometimes.

The bells on her feet, the *ghunghroos*, then pound.
And the lights in the bazaar all light up.

* A legendary slave girl, Anaarkali, fell in love with the future emperor Jehangir and was ordered to be buried alive.

# The Fire Queen of Jhansi

Preserving the objects of war, objects of worship,
pioneer woman gambling into your daredevil ways,
you slipped into the art of sword fighting in a less dark age
than ours; shooting on a target with a gun, like the eddy of stars.

Your name changed from Manu to Lakshmi Bai as you were,
strapped to a royal husband, so much for the wide sweep of your
queening, you donned the borderless mantle of widowed life,
at eighteen, when girls fill their outward hunt, with grit and pith.

Royal queen, you would stretch the bow of your single status.
While we moderns sit and argue about women going into combat,
you turned the spin of infinity to favor, the gutless enemy fled.
Dressed to disguise, your courage charred foreign bodies.

Your son Damodar tied to your back, you could use both hands,
while their breath, galloping to keep up with your two swords,
vied man to man, your resplendent talent an ironic aftertaste,
you had to fall alas, while your two and twenty years slit necks.

Tomboy queen, your fire spewed from the women's *zenana*
where you could not stay for long, broke its chains, engraved
social norms that turn hoary, shudder, wither and cringe, your
fired womanhood, a blistered, unstoppable, stringed instrument.

If a woman is a caressed toy, then you too are like one. Like a mountain, sweeping its tallness with its bodiless strength; if a woman would refuse her fate, you cry hoarse at the perjury, of life, its rubble kicked in face, while naked guns search the rubble.

* Renowned as a leader of the first war of Independence against the British, the Rani of Jhansi was more than a martial leader.

# An Old Bag Is Not An Old Hag

It was gold jewelry for her in the swelter of New Delhi,
it calmed her against the irascible nature
of love's artillery. Sunk inside the scratches of her
obsessions, like the dead cow's belly resurfacing art in
contorted calligraphy. She finds it quietly diseased now.

She sprinkles diamonds on fresh flowers, which she laces
her possible past with. The jacaranda tree smells of the bowl
of *sambar daal* and rice he threw against the same wall that
had once witnessed their playful lovemaking, soothing the soft
roundness of her lush bosom, supplicant of his deliberate strokes,
until the roundness, the lushness, the soothing, baked under his
thinning. Or hers.

Punches at the deadlines now, yesterday's deadbeat
children with thick glasses and gloomy heads pondering
against the doorway, are gone. Mudslides have all, but erased
the pearl strands of jasmine that she uses, to evoke her faith
in gutless rinds of love, close multiples of the hands that still
pluck them off every morning, one limb upon another, their flesh
lean at certain fixed places and angles.

And as if all old bags are meant to whisper advice to temples,
as well as to their priests, who would regard with some

empirical sense, or not, their sagging, creaking, humping,
aching, leaking, simpering scraps, she gets the silent treatment
when, feeding on forbidden meat and good cinema,
she is found meddlesome, like her devalued jewelry.
Or better still, she paints her wild hair a dependable color,
As if "over the hill" quotes are not meant for her. Or is that
just a tattoo? Those white jasmine pearls?

# Her Inheritance

Recall my grandmother's tired voice, *daadiji's* six o'clock evening route to the temple where she collects *halwa prasad*. Her nursery chant insistence to my brother to eat as I look on, spitting image. While he gets all his cravings, there's that unfocused pimple near my nose, suggesting plenitude. My mother feels that no decent man would fall for me, ugly daughter with the pimple; launched.

Between floating and learning, I earn my college degree, life's airborne pedigree, in the smelling dust of the baleful garage, my mother feeds my brother with her hands, inside her own crackled flesh; this is all about the pros and cons of inheriting a magically possessed childhood; she gets agitated, concerned for his final year medical exam; I bargain for an unworthy arts one.

Summer of New Delhi, spanking in its torrid unamended heat, my cousin arrives in the twenty-two years of heat in his pants. While my mother slept, he kisses me, politely slips his hand under my cotton panty. He nibbles my ear, unzips himself; he puts my hand on the torrid unamended heat of his penis; it withers when the garage dust chattered, sheds amended tears.

Married to one who earns more than the unapologetic hunger of a thousand mouths, I see his earnings pile, while he picks his nose; object to his weekend rant that spreads until it is six in the morning; I sit alone on the dining chair. I hear it again. What has your father given you? What has he done for you? He should not have sold his house. You are a failure. A wimp.

My mother lies dying, *daadiji* is long dead; I continue to live on their inheritance.

## My Papa's Conundrum: From a Daughter to her Dead Father

When you wanted to show love
you did it so well,
you would twist me out of shape,
you held me up and pronounced
upon me a greatness that I reflect
in my unkindness to you.

I do not cry when I do not want to.
I pretend that life is fine, that all of us
must die one day. So I must rejoice,
while I seal your memory in a tight grip
and load it into the sepia bag of turgid bones
that I carried to a restaurant and put down,
and my brothers refused to part from its contents.

In the evening, when we immersed that sepia
bag of bones, even your memory had become a burden.
I wore my best clothes, I tried to look beautiful
even when my beauty had fled me. I am overweight.
I hate my overweight body that you invented
along with my mother who nursed you,
filled with so much love and so much passing hate,
she too was beyond tears. Why waste them on a wasted

body that lay dead to all purpose and intent,
while you cried aloud to live again,
desperate; everyone felt that you had lived,
beyond your purpose, a small man in a large frame,
unsuccessful, even with a conundrum, almost
with everything else.

## A Daughter-in-law's Guilt

Daddy, if I were to meet you again,
I'd ask your forgiveness, for all the truths
I loved hurling at you, and you loved lapping up.

How much is not enough, for you would still forgive.
But that's not what I ask for. Forgive me in earnest,
for that means, I would be forgiven, and yet not be one.

You kept calling me your daughter, and I kept
denying it. I told you so, until you died. And so you
took your love to those waters where I drowned you.

When we fed the river that lonely bag of old bones,
when I saw your old bones disappear into the waters,
then the *shunya* descended on me.

Strangely enough, many folks would take me
for yours, and your daughters, to whom you gave
your all, were also your kin, it hurt so much to know.

Daddy, I light incense for you every morning, to abate
my anger with myself, I sometimes talk to you, and then
I remember those times you hurt me. Then comes the *shunya*.

Again, until it pesters me with its noise.

## This Mother-To-Be Visits an Abortion Clinic

Some go there after the wedding dance, and a few before.
Some desire to cut off the thread, and a few must therefore.

Some pierce nails into themselves, and others jump up and down.
Some are forced into the art of love-making; others use it to clown.

Some want only sons, and others do not care for a girl or a boy.
Some treat unwanted girls with care; most treat them as cheap toy.

Some ask themselves for simpler options, and others opt out.
Some gauge it on a moral scale, others plunge into further doubt.

Some feel remorse, but carry on with their business and a day.
Some weep, and make of themselves but an indifferent prey.

Some yearn for the piece of flesh to be born and to come alive.
Some seal time away and would only have themselves thrive.

Some believe in reproductive rights and so cut off the chain.
Some turn off the lights and lean against the window pane.

Some wear plain handcuffs, and a few see themselves handcuffed.
So why does she find herself strangely abstracted, cold puffed?

This mother-to-be invokes a spirit, refutes logic, gathers comfort.
Then finds herself visiting a graveyard, a shadow her lone consort.

She finds herself staring, an infant is newborn with every cry
Her smile gets stuck, her memory refurbishes, she lets out a sigh.

## Bollywood Goddesses

A singular procession of cautious angels swirling by,
this seeming paradise where the parade names its parts.
As fashion's pawn, gyrating flesh, the soft earth beauty,
contract sex, tears and histrionics, sparks of seeded talent.

As the passionate coquette invites him in innocent chills;
alternate this with fever pitch heat, she hunts down fabrics,
by the bitter yard. She creeps in and sidles in brilliantly fangled
folds, shortening as the years go by, figure-gripping fashions.

Just as the creeping woodbines crawl and slither, knees bent,
in forward illusion, neck to neck in transfiguring motion,
she gyrates without fuss or rest. In classic tones or modern,
a motley matching of rhythms, taxi turns with her partner.

That bell-tower known as beauty divine, she dwindles souls,
spinning love fantasies into lunatic spines; this gullible trick,
of crossed out modern technologies, shaping ordinary contours
into gut-twisting lust, brown as the tones of this mortal earth.

By turns a contract girl, or a puritan diva untouchable, she agrees
to put out for so long, sleeping on down and reaping her rewards,
with futuristic reflections of nails for objects; sensuous, suggestive,
offers a startled hug, in close contortion. A marvelous spurning.

Like a linear shadow of birds in transition, she records expertise. Artiste or artist? Propitiate progression through narrow steps, ambition's incandescent rush. Explode. Then turn to the ash of oblivion. Those yesteryears of passing glory, gloriously relished.

Like art's turgid memory.

# The Inside Passage of Sisterhood

There rests a kind of counter-ageing process, like a singing bird
whose song would blossom even as its heart gladdens; who tells
the truth as the heavy-set fruit laden on the bent branch bends,
though tell it must. Carve the bitter pill in a purple shell, dye it,
in gold or silver, make it a five feet two inch wonder, roll it up.

The usual signs of a normal pulse rate rise, like a
risen cake, breaking, into knots of air, the lip riddled
with folds, like an elemental guffaw, uncontrolled by its
own scandals, as the death of a grandfather being observed
with repressed smiles, breaking out, on the edge of a walk, as
darkness invades, the sights and sounds of bodily excretion.

No self-absorption works here, no libidinous churning
of the oven, for that which is hot is chilled to death, and
the chilled reheated in layers of monthly waiting out period.
The food rolls in and out of its culinary journey, it would rather
take issue with its own ponderous self, authentic in its essence,
though the bullet-riddled signs tell a wise and patient story.

The raw salt of marriage counseling, the ghosts cracking
through the slits jump into their skins, sage-like settling
of the fired-up blood, then breathe back, what's remaining of
resealed relationships, for healing is a political act, unsubtle,

dividend paying, lashing out truths that can never stay nude,
tongue-biting, diving, divining, skinning, the renditions loud.

As the silences between them.

## To My Mother

You bloomed over me; I did not recognize your shadow,
you struggled to protect me; I looked askance at your shade.

Mother, if you can forgive me my sin-ridden jabs at you,
those times when you cried wouldn't hurt, my jabs, now.

The tears that I cry for you now are your own tears,
the blood that you stained me in at my guilty birth.

Your blood runs rampant over me now,
its shades bloody like the color of your tears.

It mangles me in shapes and sorrows that run amuck,
sometimes bloody as blood, then like its colorless spots.

Mummy mummy mummy, my lost heart shouts,
seeking you in my mummy cries, jabbing. Pounding.

You squeezed me once so tight, your embrace smells still,
the talcum powder squeezed in your mothering armpits.

And when my typhoid fever rose so high, you sat all night,
rising to the tides of prayer, strong like your bones, stone-like.

Until I became vain, my scornful vanity its recognition point,
thrusting at you my petty jewels, glitter like my own falseness.

Your wise counsel fell on deaf ears, my deafness, false like me,
preening, weaning, maligning, satirizing, shaming, slamming.

# The Story of Indian Women, Indian Goddesses

We who share the same language,
of culture, and its benign blank spots.
We sew, we cut, we stitch up the best,
a landscape adapted incorrigibly to tears.

We are rife with them, stretching to escape,
resisting the contours, the wrinkles, the relationship,
of a lyric and its notes, the mirroring of us in it,
until time fades them, replaced, spliced, restitched.

We take the torch, through those gold fields,
of harvest wheat, for those scattered bones, bare.
We strut about, perform roles, like the odor,
of rotting wounds, measured in our prim silences.

We live in shifting rhythms of common experiences,
the grammatical swerves of common generations,
lodged in the lyric texture of common heritage,
pageantry that replaces random acts of forgiveness.

We are the twin faces, the same coin, false, genuine,
gray skies shining on gutted, muddy roads, like love,
that never lasts, yet stays smooth, often glitters, the same
jerky ground, brimming over, the same choices and chances.

We would pull taut those soiled sheets that
lie between us, and the breast-milk that drops,
between us, our daughters, and granddaughters
cast in tufts of flame or flare, anticipation, of friction.

We wear bright sunrise on our weary sleeves,
for we are a means, a fulfillment, modestly blinking,
at us, feeding our compassion to those who must,
we are own legends, birthings, burials, cremation, pregnancies.

We are the same, the everyone, the untouched Saudamini,
Gautami, Sistsuma, Urmila; Annapurna's stud;
the unwanted Mona Lisa, the bravery of Ram Dulari; we are
Indira and Sonia; we are the many loves in the *paak kothas*
of virgin Umrao Jaans, the wandering Mira, the wild
afternoons of Radha, the delightful, frightful braids
of the Medusa mother-in-law, the multiplicity of tribal love,
the wisdom of Saraswati and Gargi; we are the golden geese
for our parents, the few choices of Sita, of Allah's wife, the
flames, the tumors of deceased Sitas, the sea of Akharya,
the shimmering coral, Shehrazade; we are the bodily rhythms,
the skin colors, the call of blood, the voices; we are the
menopause of Amba, the witchcraft performed by sleeping
beauties, the labor pangs of Uma and Gauri, the widowhood
of Urvashi, the cowardice of Shakti; we are the skin painting,
the *bindis*, the ornamentation; the *sati-savitri*, the cosmopolitan,
the multicultural; we are the "rakhi" bonds of sisters, we are the
Gandharwa marriages, the killings, the banishings, the dowry
deaths, the child brides, the *sati* of Roopmati, the puppetry of
Shaswati, the mass suicide of Mohua, the myths of Mandodhari,
Kaushalya, Tishya, Shurpanakha; we are the crossovers, the
item girls, Menaka, Ambika, Sati, Manjushree, Mythili.

Our stories, dressed, then redressed. We who embrace,
The proper space. Stuttering, stumbling, shuffling,
muttering, we are the outcasts, the in-casts, the sub-castes…